EYEWITNESS ANIMALS

THE STORY OF

CHRISTMAS

The Standard Publishing Company, Cincinnati, Ohio
A division of Standex International Corporation
© 1997 by The Standard Publishing Company
All rights reserved. Printed in the United States of America.
Library of Congress Catalog Card Number 96-38394
04 03 02 01 00 99 98 97   5 4 3 2 1

Designed by Coleen Davis
Graphic layout by Dale Meyers
Edited by Greg Holder

EYEWITNESS ANIMALS

THE STORY OF
CHRISTMAS

written by
Robin Currie

illustrated by
Max Kolding

STANDARD
PUBLISHING
Cincinnati, Ohio

For Philip Ramsey – pastor, mentor, friend

CONTENTS

Long ago, Jesus was born to be the Savior of the world. It all began when an angel with good news spoke to Mary and Joseph. And a little sparrow was watching.

Tweeter Sparrow

Hi! I'm Tweeter Sparrow.

I live in a treetop in Nazareth.

Point way up in a tree.

From my tree I see up and down the street.

I can see donkeys and carts,

women carrying big jars of water,

and rich men in colorful robes.

What's your favorite color?

My story is about what I saw from my tree one day.

It was early in the morning.

I could see into the house of a girl called Mary.

She was a kind girl.

She never forgot to sprinkle the last crumbs

of her breakfast bread out for us birds.

Pretend to sprinkle some crumbs for the birds.

I perched above Mary's window.

She would be putting some crumbs out before long.

I wanted to get some before the crows came.

Say "Caw, caw!" like a crow.

When I looked into the window of Mary's house,

I forgot all about crows and crumbs!

Mary was talking to someone

I had never seen before. It was an angel!

Point to the angel in the picture.

The angel was dressed in white

and had a bright light around him.

At first Mary looked afraid.

But the angel said to her,

"Please don't be afraid.

I have good news for you."

Listen carefully so you hear the good news.

8

I had heard that Mary would be marrying

a carpenter named Joseph.

Maybe the good news was about the wedding.

But the good news surprised me so much

that I almost fell off my branch.

The angel said, "You will have a baby boy.

He will be God's Son."

Pretend to rock the baby.

Mary was going to have a baby!

But being a mommy is a lot of work for a young girl.

Who will take care of Mary and the baby? I thought.

But Mary was not worried.

She smiled and said to the angel,

"I will do what God wants me to do."

Make a big smile.

Then suddenly, the angel was gone.

Now Mary was all alone.

Later that day I saw Mary talking to Joseph.

He looked very sad.

Make a sad face.

Maybe Joseph could not help Mary

take care of God's Son.

When Joseph left, I flew overhead

and watched him walk slowly

back to his carpenter's shop.

He lay down on his bed and went to sleep.

Rest head on hands.

Early the next morning

I followed Joseph to Mary's house.

He seemed to be in a big hurry.

He knocked on Mary's door.

Knock, knock, knock.

When she came out he said,

"Last night an angel talked to me in a dream.

He told me that I should take care of you

and the baby you will have.

He will be God's own Son.

We will call him Jesus."

Clap your hands.

Mary smiled.

God would give her a baby

and someone to take care of them both.

Smile really big.

A little sparrow would not fly all the way to Bethlehem with Mary and Joseph, but a donkey could carry them all the way there.

Clomper Donkey

Hello there!

My name is Clomper Donkey.

Hee-haw!

I'm an old donkey, so I'm a little slow.

I belong to a carpenter named Joseph.

Carpenters make things out of wood.

Joseph makes chairs and beds for people's houses

and wheels for their horse carts.

I help him carry his wood and tools.

Joseph's favorite tools are his hammer and saw.

Pretend to hammer and saw.

He is a very hard worker.

We have worked together for a long time,

but now things at his house have changed.

He has a new young wife named Mary.

Point to Mary in the picture.

Sometimes I help her carry water from the well.

And she never forgets to bring me a carrot

when she comes to the carpenter shop.

Rub your tummy.

My story is about a long trip

that Joseph, Mary, and I took together.

Point to yourself.

It didn't seem like a very good time to travel.

As Joseph packed bags of clothing on me

I said to my friend Tweeter Sparrow,

"Why are they taking a trip this time of year?

The roads are crowded and everyone is in a hurry."

But Tweeter said that all the humans

had to travel to their hometown

to be counted by the Romans.

How high can you count?

Joseph's hometown was called Bethlehem.

So Mary and Joseph had to travel

all the way to Bethlehem to be counted.

Point a long way away.

So the bags were packed on my back.

Mary came out and Joseph helped her on my back, too.

That was very strange.

Mary usually walked with Joseph.

But I noticed how tired she looked,

and I didn't mind, even though my load was heavy.

I'm an old donkey, so we couldn't go very fast.

Tap your hand slowly on your knees.

The road was crowded.

Fast chariots with Roman soldiers zoomed by us.

Children were playing games beside the road.

What's your favorite outside game?

Lots of people were walking toward Bethlehem.

Once a woman spoke to Mary.

She said, "This is a bad time for you to travel.

Your baby could be born any time now."

Fold your arms to rock the baby.

I thought to myself,

What if the baby was born on our trip?

I had to get Mary to Bethlehem right away.

I started clomping along

as fast as my old legs could carry us.

We didn't pass up any Roman chariots,

but Joseph had to walk quickly to keep up with me.

Tap your hands quickly on your knees.

It took us a long time to get to Bethlehem,

but we finally made it!

Everyone was tired from our long trip.

Yawn.

As we entered the town of Bethlehem,

Joseph started to look worried about Mary.

Maybe the baby was coming soon.

Maybe tonight!

Hee-haw!

A donkey could not find a place to stay in a strange town, but a kitty cat would know her way around.

Fluffy Kitty

Hello! I'm Fluffy Kitty.

I belong to an innkeeper in Bethlehem.

Meow.

An inn is a place where people can sleep

when they are visiting from out of town.

Pretend to take a nap.

The innkeeper gave me a very important job.

I keep the mice out of the kitchen.

I have to rest all day and evening

so I can stay up all night chasing mice.

Say "Squeak!" like a little mouse.

My story is about one evening

when the inn was very crowded.

I tried lying in front of the fire,

but I couldn't get much sleep.

People were everywhere!

I finally found a place to lie down

right outside the front door of the inn.

Everyone else was inside, so I could get some sleep.

Yawn like you are sleepy.

Just as I closed my eyes, I heard a sound.

It sounded like a donkey walking very slowly.

Tap your hands on your knees very slowly.

In the dim light I could see

a man and a woman with their old donkey.

They knocked on the door of another inn

that was down the road.

Knock, knock, knock.

The man said, "Do you have any room?"

Then someone came to the door and said,

"Not tonight. All of our rooms are full."

The donkey could hardly lift his feet anymore,

but the woman spoke softly to him

and he clomped on down the road.

The man knocked on another door.

Knock, knock, knock.

"Do you have any room?" called the man.

Someone came to the door and said,

"Tonight you won't find an empty room

anywhere in Bethlehem! Now go away!"

Point away from you.

The man and woman continued down the road

and stopped right in front of *my* inn.

The man knocked on the door.

Knock, knock, knock.

The innkeeper was too busy to answer,

so his wife came to the door instead.

"Oh, dear," she said.

"We don't have a corner to spare.

Every bed and table and chair is full."

Just then the woman on the donkey sighed.

She was so tired.

Sigh and pretend you are sleepy.

The innkeeper's wife looked up and said,

"Oh my! You're almost ready to have a baby!"

Fold your arms to rock the baby.

If this woman was going to have a baby,

I knew just the right place for them to stay.

The stable behind the inn was the same place

I had my kittens last spring.

It was nice and warm inside the stable,

and they could sleep on the soft hay.

It was up to me to show them where to go.

So I jumped up and began to meow.

Meow.

"What is it, Fluffy Kitty?"

asked the innkeeper's wife.

I meowed and waved my tail again.

Meow, meow, meow!

The woman on the donkey said,

"I think your cat wants us to follow her."

I led them behind the inn and right to the stable.

The man said, "This will be just fine.

No one will bother us back here,

and the hay is clean and soft."

The woman said, "Thank you, Fluffy Kitty,"

and scratched behind my ears.

Say "Thank you, Fluffy Kitty!"

Now that this nice man and woman had a place to stay,

maybe I would finally get some sleep!

Meow.

A cat could not perch on the manger and see everything that was going on, but a cricket could.

Chirpy Cricket

Hi-hi-hi!

I'm Chirpy Cricket.

I live in a stable in Bethlehem.

A stable is a small barn where animals live.

When the moon comes out,

I sing and make music all night long

by rubbing my wings together.

Chip-chirrup!

My stable is a nice home.

I live here with a dove and two cows.

Say "coo" like a dove and "moo" like a cow.

On most nights we don't have any visitors.

But I want to tell you about one night

when we *did* have some special visitors.

Who do you think it was?

That night, the moon was just coming up.

I was getting ready to sing my cricket song

when I heard footsteps outside the stable.

Tap your hands on your knees very slowly.

The door creaked open

and a man and a woman stepped inside.

"Look, Mary," the man said with a smile.

"We can sleep here tonight."

Here? In our stable? I thought.

We've never had people *sleep in our stable before.*

The man and woman must have been very tired,

because soon they were sleeping quietly in the hay.

That sounded like a good idea,

and so I curled up in the warm hay and shut my eyes.

I can wait and sing my song tomorrow night, I thought.

Later on that night,

A strange new noise woke me up.

Stretch your arms in the air like you just woke up.

The noise wasn't a man or a woman.

And I was *sure* it wasn't one of the other animals.

"What was that?" I chirped.

One of the cows said,

"That's the sound of a brand new baby."

I hopped up on the side of the manger to get a look.

The cow was right! It *was* a brand new baby!

Fold your arms to rock the baby.

The woman wrapped the baby in blankets

and laid him in the manger right beside me.

He sure is a little guy, I thought.

"Go to sleep now, little Jesus," said the woman.

She began to hum a little song for him.

Can you hum your favorite song?

I can sing for the baby, too, I thought.

So I rubbed my wings together

and sang right along.

Chip-chirrup!

The woman smiled when she heard my song.

I looked down into the manger

and the little baby was smiling, too!

I was so happy, I could have sung all night!

But before very long, the baby closed his eyes

and was fast asleep in his manger bed.

Soon the only noise was the baby's soft breathing

and a very quiet cricket lullaby.

Chip-chirrup!

A cricket could not travel out to the sheep fields, but a shepherd boy's puppy would be right at home there.

Yip-yap Puppy

Hi!

I'm Yip-yap Puppy.

I belong to a little shepherd boy

in a field outside of Bethlehem.

Yip-yip-yap!

I'm not big enough to really guard the sheep yet.

And my boy is not big enough to watch them.

Shake your head.

But we go along with the other shepherds
and their dogs so we can learn what to do.
One day we'll be big enough.

Point to yourself.

My story takes place after a busy day in the field.

My boy and I had played in the sun for hours.

Sometimes we had to run after a little lamb

that had wandered away from its mother.

Baaa.

When night came, it was time for bed.

We wanted to stay up all night

and watch the sheep, but we weren't allowed.

One day we'll be big enough.

Point to yourself.

My boy rolled up in a blanket

and we looked up at the stars.

Point to the stars in the sky.

Maybe if we stayed awake all night

the other shepherds would think

we were big enough to guard the flock.

But the stars made us so sleepy

that soon my boy and I were sound asleep.

Rest your head on your hands.

Suddenly, we heard the shepherds shouting.

We both jumped up, wide awake.

What happened? I wondered.

Is there a wolf? Or a lion?

But it wasn't an animal that scared the shepherds.

They were looking at an angel in the sky.

Point up to the sky.

42

The angel said, "A new king is born.

He is sleeping in a barn in Bethlehem."

My boy held me close and said,

"Yip-yap, a barn is for cows and doves,

but not for babies."

Where do babies usually sleep?

Then the angel said,

"Go to Bethlehem and see the new king!"

Suddenly the sky was full of angels

singing praises to God.

It was the most beautiful music in the world.

Sing your favorite song about Jesus.

I howled right along with them!

Yow-yow-yow!

Suddenly it was over.

The lights and voices and singing were gone.

43

When it was over, shepherds talked

about what they had just seen.

They asked each other,

"What should we do? What should we do?"

Shrug.

But my boy and I knew what to do.

He said, "Let's go to Bethlehem

and find the baby king!"

Clap your hands.

I barked to show I agreed.

Yip-yip-yap!

So everyone started running to Bethlehem.

My boy and I got to lead the way

because it was our idea.

We were big enough to do that!

Point to yourself.

A dog might be too noisy around a baby, but a little lamb could go quietly inside the stable with the shepherds.

Woolsey Lamb

Hello.

I'm Woolsey Lamb.

Baa-baa.

I live in a big field with lots of other sheep.

Since I'm a brand new baby,

I need to be with my mama

and a brave shepherd all the time.

Pretend to hold a baby lamb very close.

My story is about the night I took my first trip

away from the field and into the town of Bethlehem.

We were all sleeping peacefully,

 when suddenly there was a bright light in the sky.

Point to the sky.

I heard talking and singing,

but I didn't understand what was happening.

When the night was quiet and dark again,

the shepherds got ready to leave.

One of them was my special shepherd.

He had been taking care of me since I was born.

He gathered me into his arms and said,

"I guess you will come with us, Woolsey Lamb.

You are too little to leave out here in the cold."

Shiver and pretend you are cold.

I didn't know where we were going this late at night.

It was way past my bedtime and I was still sleepy.

When is your bedtime?

But when I saw that Mama was coming with us

I knew everything was all right.

My shepherd carried me all the way to Bethlehem.

As soon as we got into town,

we stopped at the first house we saw.

The shepherds knocked on the door and asked,

"Where is the new baby king?"

Touch your fingertips overhead to make a house.

A man opened the door and said,

"There is no new baby in this house."

Shake your head.

We stopped at the second house.

The shepherds knocked on the door and asked,

"Where is the new baby king?"

Touch your fingertips overhead to make a house.

A woman opened the door and said,

"There is no new baby in this house.

Shake your head.

We stopped at the third house.

The shepherd knocked on the door and asked,

"Where is the new baby king?"

Touch your fingertips overhead to make a house.

A little girl opened the door and said,

"There is no new baby here,

but I thought I heard a baby's cry

coming from that stable a while ago ."

The shepherds tiptoed to the stable and looked inside.

"Where is the new baby king?" they asked.

A man said, "My name is Joseph,

and the baby king is right here in the stable."

Shout "Hooray!" and clap your hands.

The baby was sleeping in the hay,

just like the angels had told them.

Soon it was time to return to the fields.

But the shepherds did not go back there right away.

They stopped at each house and said,

"A new baby king is born."

And even though I was a very little lamb,

I had seen the new king, too.

Baa-baa.

A lamb could not travel for days on the hot sand, but a camel could carry important visitors to Bethlehem.

Sandy Camel

Hello there!

I'm Sandy Camel.

I live in a land very far away from Bethlehem.

I belong to a wise man who works in a king's palace.

We go on lots of long trips together.

Where would you like to go on a trip?

My story is about a long trip we took

to see a new baby king.

It all started one night when we were

outside looking at the stars.

Suddenly my master pointed to the sky and said,

"Look at that bright new star.

It means a new king has been born!"

I looked up into the night sky,

but all the stars looked the same to me.

Pretend to look at the stars.

My master rushed back inside the palace

to tell the other wise men about the star.

When he finished, one of them said,

"We should go and find this new king

so we can worship him and give him gifts."

They decided to travel together to find the baby king.

The next day we started our journey.

First we had to cross a sandy desert.

The sun was hot and there was no water anywhere.

Pretend it's hot and fan yourself with your hand.

It's a good thing camels don't get thirsty very often!

Next we traveled across some big mountains.

My legs got tired from climbing so much,

but I kept walking until we reached the other side.

Pretend you are climbing something very tall.

On and on we went until we came to Jerusalem.

One of the wise men said,

"This is a big city with many important people.

Surely someone will know about the new king."

The wise men went to see King Herod and asked him,

"Where can we find the new baby king?"

But Herod did not know.

Shake your head.

Then Herod asked his teachers and priests

where the baby king could be found.

They opened their scrolls and said,

"The new baby king was born in Bethlehem."

Pretend to read from a scroll.

So we left Jerusalem and headed for Bethlehem.

While we were traveling down the road,

an amazing thing happened.

The special star appeared in the sky again—

and it was moving!

Pretend to point to the star.

The wise men were very happy.

We followed the star to a little house in Bethlehem.

Outside there was a man and a woman

playing with a little boy.

As soon as the wise men saw the boy,

they bowed low to the ground.

Can you bow low like the wise men?

Then they gave him wonderful gifts

that were fit for a king.

What gift would you give the baby king?

Years later, Jesus grew up to become
a very important man. He showed people
how to love each other and how to please God.

The reason we celebrate Christmas
is not to get lots of toys, although that's lots of fun.
The real reason for Christmas is to celebrate
the birth of Jesus, God's Son!

That's Good News for Christmas and every day!